Ba

Wholeness

Scripture text:
> All Scripture quotations are taken from the Holy Bible,
> New International Version (copyright 1973, 1978, 1984,
> International Bible Society), unless otherwise indicated.

Additional Text:
> Melanie Jongsma
> Copyright 1992, The Bible League

Published by

THE BIBLE LEAGUE

16801 Van Dam Road • South Holland, Illinois 60473, USA

Box 5037, Burlington, Ontario, L7R 3Y8, Canada

Box 464, Penrith, NSW 2751, Australia

Box 77-047, Mt. Albert, New Zealand

Printed in U.S.A.

A100-61

Do not be far from me,
for trouble is near
and there is no one to help.
(Psalm 22:11)

[The Lord] has not despised or disdained
the suffering of the afflicted one;
he has not hidden his face from him
but has listened to his cry for help.
(Psalm 22:24)

New Beginnings

You may feel
like it's all over for you.

The things you've been forced to live through
have left you used-up,
weak,
and lost.

You've been the victim
of someone else's choices,
      abused,
      abandoned,
      broken down,
      by people you should have been able to trust.
And now you can't even make yourself believe
in second chances.

But don't give up.

God
is a God of new beginnings.

This God
whose compassionate power healed the sick
and even restored the dead
can bring new life
to your tired, trampled-on, hopeless soul.

In a broken-down world
of closed doors
and dead ends,
he
can give you
the fresh start you need.

[God] gives strength to the weary
and increases the power of the weak.
Even youths grow tired and weary,
and young men stumble and fall;
but those who hope in the Lord will renew their strength.
They will soar on wings like eagles;
they will run and not grow weary,
they will walk and not be faint.
(Isaiah 40:29-31)

Therefore,
if anyone is in Christ,
he is a new creation;
the old has gone,
the new has come!
(2 Corinthians 5:17)

No Matter What

No matter what you've gone through,
no matter who's done what to you,
God's love can heal you.

Pain and ugliness come in many different forms
through many different people,
and much of the pain that is forced into our lives
is senseless and unfair.

So many things that we have no control over
seem to have the power
to steal our dreams,
ruin our plans,
and drain us of the joy and normalcy
that most people take for granted.

But God's love
is stronger
deeper
bigger
than anything
in this world, this life.

He can restore us
no matter where we are
or how we hurt.

In the face of your suffering,
in the heart of your pain,
reach out to believe
that
his love can free you,
and his grace can change you—

no matter what.

I pray that out of his glorious riches he may strengthen you with power through his Spirit in your inner being, so that Christ may dwell in your hearts through faith. And I pray that you, being rooted and established in love, may have power, together with all the saints, to grasp how wide and long and high and deep is the love of Christ, and to know this love that surpasses knowledge—that you may be filled to the measure of all the fullness of God.

(Ephesians 3:16-19)

For I am convinced
that neither death nor life,
neither angels nor demons,
neither the present nor the future,
nor any powers,
neither height nor depth,
nor anything else in all creation
will be able to separate us from the love of God
that is in Christ Jesus our Lord.

(Romans 8:38-39)

You grant [me] relief from days of trouble,
till a pit is dug for the wicked.
For the Lord will not reject his people;
he will never forsake his inheritance. . . .

Jim Whitmer

Unless the Lord had given me help,
I would soon have dwelt in the silence of death.
When I said, "My foot is slipping,"
your love, O Lord, supported me.
When anxiety was great within me,
your consolation brought joy to my soul.
(Psalm 94:13-19)

Doubt and Trust

Where was God
> *when I was being hurt?*
> *I cried out to him every day—*
> *didn't he hear me?*
> *Didn't he care?*
> *How could he let my suffering go on?*
> *How could he leave me alone?*

Your doubts about God are real.
And God
knows them . . .
> and accepts them.

Don't be afraid to express yourself to God.
He will not be shocked
> by the fierceness of your anger
> or the depth of your despair.
In fact, he's had all those feelings himself.
He will listen to your struggles
and show you the way
back to strength.

God understands.

In the midst of all your apprehensions
you can slowly learn
to reach out to him.

It's OK
to doubt him
and trust him
at the same time.

About the ninth hour Jesus cried out in a loud voice, . . .
"My God, my God, why have you forsaken me?"
(Matthew 27:46)

How long, O Lord? Will you forget me forever?
How long will you hide your face from me?
How long must I wrestle with my thoughts
and every day have sorrow in my heart?
How long will my enemy triumph over me?

Look on me and answer, O Lord my God.
Give light to my eyes, or I will sleep in death;
my enemy will say, "I have overcome him,"
and my foes will rejoice when I fall.

But I trust in your unfailing love;
my heart rejoices in your salvation.
I will sing to the Lord,
for he has been good to me.
(Psalm 13)

Numbness

No words could describe the injuries that scar you
inside and out.

Even if you could talk about them
you wouldn't.
This heavy numbness is your only protection
from memories
and fears
and a horror that doesn't even seem quite real
anymore.

Maybe your cloak of darkness
keeps you from reaching out to God—
                    Have you given up talking to him
                    because you don't know what to say?

Don't worry about the words.

When all you have is the numbness
around your pain,
God's Spirit helps you.
He endures your struggles
and senses your feelings,
and actually does your praying for you,

          expressing the hurts you can't bear to feel

                    and pleading to God on your behalf.

The Spirit [of God] helps us in our weakness. We do not know what we ought to pray for, but the Spirit himself intercedes for us with groans that words cannot express. And he who searches our hearts knows the mind of the Spirit, because the Spirit intercedes for the saints in accordance with God's will.
(Romans 8:26-27)

Help for the Helpless

Are you the victim of someone else's anger
or addiction
or feelings of inadequacy?

Have you been trapped into dependence on someone
who takes advantage of you
again and again?

Maybe your reality is made up of
lies and broken promises
and no-win situations,
and the only way you ever feel
is
helpless.

To make matters worse,
even friends
can't understand why you don't just <u>do</u> something
about your problems.
The self-reliance and independence they take for granted
make them frustrated with your uncertainty
and confused by your powerlessness.
In trying to offer help and advice,
they only make you feel even more
overwhelmed.

You are not to blame
for the hurts others cause you.

Try to keep believing
that there is
        a way out.

Those who trust in God are never helpless.

I lift up my eyes to the hills—
where does my help come from?
My help comes from the Lord,
the Maker of heaven and earth.
He will not let your foot slip—
he who watches over you will not slumber;
indeed, he who watches over Israel
will neither slumber nor sleep.

(Psalm 121:1-4)

I can do everything
through him who gives me strength.

(Philippians 4:13)

Why, O Lord, do you stand far off?
Why do you hide yourself in times of trouble?
In his arrogance the wicked man hunts down the weak,
who are caught in the schemes he devises.
His ways are always prosperous;
he is haughty and your laws are far from him;
he sneers at all his enemies.
He says to himself, "Nothing will shake me;
I'll always be happy and never have trouble."
His mouth is full of curses and lies and threats;
trouble and evil are under his tongue.
He lies in wait near the villages;
from ambush he murders the innocent,
watching in secret for his victims.
He lies in wait like a lion in cover;
he lies in wait to catch the helpless;
he catches the helpless and drags them off in his net.
His victims are cursed, they collapse;
they fall under his strength.
He says to himself, "God has forgotten;
he covers his face and never sees."

Jim Whitmer

But you, O God, do see trouble and grief;
you consider it to take it in hand.
The victim commits himself to you;
you are the helper of the fatherless.
Break the arm of the wicked and evil man;
call him to account
for his wickedness that would not be found out.

The Lord is King forever and ever;
the nations will perish from his land.
You hear, O Lord, the desire of the afflicted;
you encourage them, and you listen to their cry,
defending the fatherless and the oppressed,
in order that man, who is of the earth, may terrify no more.
(Psalm 10:1-2, 5-11, 14-18)

How Long?

Sometimes it seems
as if you have never felt anything
but anguish
frustration
and fear.

Sometimes it seems
as if once you've been victimized by someone
you are always under his power,
and your life is never your own again.

How long does pain last?

When will I be one of the "normal" people?

Why won't the hurting stop?

God hears your cries.

He has always heard the cries of his children.

And he has always reached out

to save them.

Be merciful to me, Lord, for I am faint;
O Lord, heal me, for my bones are in agony.
My soul is in anguish.
How long, O Lord, how long?

Turn, O Lord, and deliver me;
save me because of your unfailing love.
No one remembers you when he is dead.
Who praises you from the grave?

I am worn out from groaning;
all night long I flood my bed with weeping
and drench my couch with tears.
My eyes grow weak with sorrow;
they fail because of all my foes.

Away from me, all you who do evil,
for the Lord has heard my weeping.
The Lord has heard my cry for mercy;
the Lord accepts my prayer.
All my enemies will be ashamed and dismayed;
they will turn back in sudden disgrace.

(Psalm 6:2-10)

Give ear to my words,
O Lord,
consider my sighing.
Listen to my cry for help,
my King and my God,
for to you I pray.
In the morning, O Lord, you hear my voice;
in the morning I lay my requests before you
and wait in expectation.

(Psalm 5:1-3)

Jim Whitmer

But let all who take refuge in you be glad;
let them ever sing for joy.
Spread your protection over them,
that those who love your name may rejoice in you.
For surely, O Lord, you bless the righteous;
you surround them with your favor
as with a shield.

(Psalm 5:11-12)

Wait and See

Too often it's true
that bad things happen to good people.

While God gives each of us
a certain measure of control over our lives,
the consequences
life sometimes deals us
don't always match the choices we make.
Bad things happen to good people.
Life isn't
fair.

Why?

Our world is torn between opposing forces;
and while God is the ultimate ruler,
there is
an Enemy,
an Evil Power,
who desperately struggles
to wrestle our lives
out of God's hand
and ruin his plans
for us, his children.

That's why
innocence dies
and dreams turn to dust.
That's why life isn't fair
and bad things happen to good people.

But God *is*
in control.

It may seem
sometimes
that he's no longer interested,
that he's left the world
to wearily
spin
itself
into
hopeless ashes,
while a million fearless demons
dance in victory.

But things are not always
what they seem.
God is at work to bind those singing demons
and restore this fallen world
to its potential glory.
In spite of how things look now,
God
is in control.

Maybe someday
when we step back
and see
his grand universal plan,
with all the players in place,
and all the strategies revealed,
we'll understand
why bad things happen.

For now, though,
we can only wait
and believe.

For Example

Maybe you've heard of Job;
his story is in the Bible.

Job was a good man.
He went to church every day.
He was generous and fair in his business dealings.
He held a position of respect in the government.
And he kept all of God's laws.

Even so, Job, one day,
lost all of his wealth to vandals,
all of his children to violent deaths,
and was himself struck down with a painful and ugly illness.
Everything he had was turned to ashes.

God *let* him suffer
                    for a reason he couldn't see.

Here's how he reacted:

> "How I long for the months gone by,
> for the days when God watched over me,
> when his lamp shone upon my head
> and by his light I walked through darkness!
> . . . I cry out to you, O God, but you do not answer;
> I stand up, but you merely look at me.
> You turn on me ruthlessly;
> with the might of your hand you attack me.
> You snatch me up and drive me before the wind;
> you toss me about in the storm.
> I know you will bring me down to death,
> to the place appointed for all the living."
> (Job 29:2-3; 30:20-23)

And here's how God responded:

> "Where were you when I laid the earth's foundation?. . .
> Will the one who contends with the Almighty correct him?
> Let him who accuses God answer him!"
> (Job 38:4, 40:1)

Then Job answered the Lord:

> "I am unworthy—how can I reply to you?
> . . . Surely I spoke of things I did not understand,
> things too wonderful for me to know."
> (Job 40:4; 42:3)

After years of wondering, *"But **why**, Lord?"*,
Job finally came to realize
that he didn't have to know the answers
to the problem of his pointless pain.
He only had to believe, *"God loves me. And I trust him."*

And, having passed the test,
he found the peace he needed
and was blessed with greater riches than he'd ever imagined.

The same will happen for us
as we choose to expand our trust in God
beyond our own, human perception. For—

> "No eye has seen,
> no ear has heard,
> no mind has conceived
> what God has prepared for those who love him."
> (1 Corinthians 2:9)

Praise be to the God and Father of our Lord Jesus Christ! In his great mercy he has given us new birth into a living hope through the resurrection of Jesus Christ from the dead, and into an inheritance that can never perish, spoil or fade—kept in heaven for you, who through faith are shielded by God's power until the coming of the salvation that is ready to be revealed in the last time. In this you greatly rejoice, though now for a little while you may have had to suffer grief in all kinds of trials.

(1 Peter 1:3-6)

Jim Whitmer

27

Righteous Anger

Believe it or not,
God is **angry**
about the misery you're in.

He's not a passive, emotionless God
who answers your outrage with,
"Calm down and trust me."

He's not detached from the world
or indifferent to your heartaches.
He knows it's unfair.

And he's angry.

God never planned for people
to use and hurt and scar each other.
He will not tolerate injustice.

His rage will ignite
and his anger will burn,

and the earth will shake with his wrath.

The earth trembled and quaked,
and the foundations of the mountains shook;
they trembled because [God] was angry.
. . . He reached down from on high and took hold of me;
he drew me out of deep waters.
He rescued me from my powerful enemy,
from my foes, who were too strong for me.
They confronted me in the day of my disaster,
but the Lord was my support.
He brought me out into a spacious place;
he rescued me because he delighted in me.
(Psalm 18:7,16-19)

Though my father and mother forsake me,
the Lord will receive me.
(Psalm 27:10)

O Lord my God, I take refuge in you;
save and deliver me from all who pursue me . . .
Arise, O Lord, in your anger;
rise up against the rage of my enemies.
Awake, my God; decree justice.

(Psalm 7:1,6)

Jim Whitmer

Jesus said to his disciples:
"Things that cause people to sin are
bound to come,
but woe to that person
through whom they come.
It would be better for him to be thrown
into the sea
with a millstone tied
around his neck
than for him to cause one of these
little ones
to sin."
(Luke 17:1-2)

"See that you do not look down
on one of these little ones.
For I tell you
that their angels in heaven
always
see the face of my Father in heaven."
(Matthew 18:10-11)

Where to Turn

If you
are an innocent victim
of this world's worst nightmares,
you,
at the very least,
are probably questioning
your relationship with God.

You may feel that he doesn't understand you,
or that he's not as real as you need him to be,
or that he just doesn't care.

But this God has suffered just as you have.
He, too, was an innocent victim
of abuse and anger
hatred and humiliation
false charges and overwhelming odds.
He never deserved his pain.

You may be
confident
       in God's life-changing power
or confused
       by his apparent silence—
you may understand him
or you may not,

          but still, he *is* the only answer to your pain.

Turn to *God*.

He's the only source
of healing
     peace
         and new life.

[Christ] was despised and rejected by men,
a man of sorrows, and familiar with suffering.
Like one from whom men hide their faces
he was despised, and we esteemed him not.
Surely he took up our infirmities and carried our sorrows,
. . . he was pierced for our transgressions,
      he was crushed for our iniquities;
. . . he was oppressed and afflicted,
. . . he was led like a lamb to the slaughter,
. . . [yet] he did not open his mouth.
(Isaiah 53:3-7)

Answer me when I call to you, O my righteous God.
Give me relief from my distress;
be merciful to me and hear my prayer.
(Psalm 4:1)

Cast your cares on the Lord and he will sustain you.
(Psalm 55:22)

But How?

Whether or not *you* know *him,*
God
already
knows
you.

He is already aware of your particular misery,
your unanswered questions,
your struggles, anger, and fear.
He's already *been* where you *are.*

He knows you're afraid
of taking on a whole new life,
even though your old one,
you admit,
is miserable.
He knows you can't quite make yourself believe that he's real.

After a lifetime
of brushing past God,
not taking him seriously,
or perhaps looking for him in all the wrong places,
you may find it hard
to confront him now face to face.

Nevertheless,
God is real.
He's not a religious theory or a vague "higher power."
He's a living, listening person,
consciously aware of the very specific you
and all your untold pain.

If you are serious about finding God,
all you have to do is look for him.

He's right here.

You created my inmost being;
you knit me together in my mother's womb.
. . . My frame was not hidden from you
when I was made in the secret place.
When I was woven together in the depths of the earth,
your eyes saw my unformed body.
All the days ordained for me
were written in your book
before one of them came to be.
(Psalm 139:13-16)

The Lord is near to all who call on him,
to all who call on him in truth.
He fulfills the desires of those who fear him;
he hears their cry
and saves them.
The Lord watches over all who love him . . . .
(Psalm 145:18-20)

Anyone who comes to him must believe that he exists
and that he rewards those who earnestly seek him.
(Hebrews 11:6)

Where can I go from your Spirit?
Where can I flee from your presence?
If I go up to the heavens, you are there;
if I make my bed in the depths, you are there.
If I rise on the wings of the dawn,
if I settle on the far side of the sea,
even there your hand will guide me,
your right hand will hold me fast.
(Psalm 139:7-10)

God is our refuge and strength,
an ever-present help in trouble.
Therefore we will not fear,
though the earth give way
and the mountains fall into the heart of the sea,
though its waters roar and foam
and the mountains quake with their surging.
. . . The Lord Almighty is with us;
the God of Jacob is our fortress.
(Psalm 46:1-7)

Jim Whitmer

[Jesus said,] "Come to me, all you who are weary and burdened, and I will give you rest. Take my yoke upon you and learn from me, for I am gentle and humble in heart, and you will find rest for your souls."

(Matthew 11:28-29)

That First Step

Perhaps you sense, somehow,
that God
is the peace
the power
the healing
you've been looking for
all your life.

Perhaps you're ready now
to try
to give him a chance.

Of course you don't understand everything about him.
                    No one does.

And you may not fully realize his plan for your life.
                    You don't have to.

Maybe you're not even sure you're ready to completely trust him.
                    It's alright.

Simply standing before him,
as nothing but the person you are—
afraid, confused, exhausted, and scarred—
is the first step
in letting him teach you
                        how
                            to
                                let
                                    go.

Humble yourselves, therefore, under God's mighty hand, that he may lift you up in due time. Cast all your anxiety on him because he cares for you.

(1 Peter 5:6-7)

Submit yourselves, then, to God. . . .
Come near to God and he will come near to you. . . .
Humble yourselves before the Lord, and he will lift you up.

(James 4:7-10)

Breaking the Ice

If you're not used to talking with God,
breaking the ice can be difficult.

> *How do I start?*

> *What do I say?*

> *How do I know if this is for real?*

Like any relationship,
a relationship with God will go through stages—
from acquaintance
to friendship
to serious commitment.
Your trust will grow
with each step you take
and you'll become more and more comfortable
with who God is
and who you are.

But
like any relationship,
the hardest part
is breaking the ice.

Some tips?
Be honest.
Be yourself.
Be sincere.

And *believe*
that
God
is
really
listening.

I sought the Lord, and he answered me;
he delivered me from all my fears.
This poor man called, and the Lord heard him;
he saved him out of all his troubles.
The eyes of the Lord are on the righteous
and his ears are attentive to their cry . . . .
The righteous cry out, and the Lord hears them;
he delivers them from all their troubles.
The Lord is close to the brokenhearted
and saves those who are crushed in spirit.

(Psalm 34, selected verses)

The Lord has heard my cry for mercy;
the Lord accepts my prayer.

(Psalm 6:9)

But we have this treasure in jars of clay to show that this all-surpassing power is from God and not from us.
We are hard pressed on every side, but not crushed;
perplexed, but not in despair;
persecuted, but not abandoned;
struck down, but not destroyed.
We always carry around in our body the death of Jesus, so that the life of Jesus may also be revealed in our body.
(2 Corinthians 4:7-10)

Jim Whitmer

This poor man called,
and the Lord heard him;
he saved him
out of all his troubles.
The angel of the Lord
encamps
around those who fear him,
and he delivers them.
(Psalm 34:6-7)

Hear my cry, O God;
listen to my prayer.

From the ends of the earth
I call to you,
I call as my heart grows faint;
lead me to the rock that is higher than I . . . .

I long to dwell in your tent forever
and take refuge in the shelter of your wings.
(Psalm 61:1-4)

the Family of God

God never leaves us stranded.

When you decide to trust God with your life,
when you accept his love for you,
you become a part of his family.

And all of us in that family
are given special gifts and talents
which we are told to use
to *be* Christ
to all the lonely, hurting people
in our lonely, hurting world.

If you are lost in brokenness and confusion,
if you are smothering in numbness and fear,
if you want to know the love of God in practical, human ways—

reach out to his people.

Counselors, pastors, and good Christian friends,
can show you
the mercy and healing,
the wisdom and patience,
the goodness
and *love*
of
God.

Why not join the Family?

Just as each of us has one body with many members, and these members do not all have the same function, so in Christ we who are many form one body, and each member belongs to all the others. We have different gifts, according to the grace given us. If a man's gift is prophesying, let him use it in proportion to his faith. If it is serving, let him serve; if it is teaching, let him teach; if it is encouraging, let him encourage; if it is contributing to the needs of others, let him give generously; if it is leadership, let him govern diligently; if it is showing mercy, let him do it cheerfully.

(Romans 12:4-8)

All the believers were together and had everything in common. Selling their possessions and goods, they gave to anyone as he had need.

(Acts 2:44-45)

a Prayer

Dear God, help me.

I'm tired of feeling battered and insignificant.
I'm tired of broken promises and misplaced trust.
God, there's nothing in my life that is stable and dependable and
good.

Will you really love me—
       no matter what other people tell me?
      no matter where I try to run?
      no matter who I think I am?
Can I really trust you with my heart?

I'm starting to understand
that I need you,
that only you
have the power to cleanse me of my past
and give me hope for my future.
Only you can save me from the pain that fills my life.

Jesus, you died for me
to give me another chance,
to offer me a way out of this world's disappointments.
I want to accept that gift now.

Please hear me, Lord, and take over my life.

Give me the strength to trust you completely.

And help me become the new person
you've promised I can be.

Thank you, Lord.

Amen.

His divine power has given us
everything we need
for life and godliness
through our knowledge of him who called us by his own glory
and goodness. Through these he has given us his very great
and precious promises, so that through them you may
participate in the divine nature
and escape
the corruption in the world caused by evil desires.

(2 Peter 1:3-4)

This booklet was given to you by:

(PJ) PEARL D JACKSON

If you would like more information
or additional copies
please contact us.

If you would like some help in establishing a daily time to
meet with God by reading his Word, write to the address
below and request a copy of the pamphlet entitled,
"Grounded in the Word." This pamphlet, a free gift from
The Bible League, will provide you with a structured guide
through the Bible, prescribing a specific Scripture passage
to read each day. Send your request to:

THE BIBLE LEAGUE

16801 Van Dam Road • South Holland, IL 60473
USA

—

P.O. Box 5037 • Burlington, Ontario, L7R 3Y8
CANADA

—

P.O. Box 464 • Penrith • NSW 2751
AUSTRALIA

—

P.O. Box 77-047 • Mt. Albert
NEW ZEALAND

and please mark the envelope "ATTN: GITW Offer"